How to Wallpaper

D1707700

WALLABY

A WALLABY BOOK
Published by Simon & Schuster
New York

Published by WALLABY BOOKS
A Simon & Schuster Division of
GULF & WESTERN CORPORATION
Simon & Schuster Building
1230 Avenue of the Americas
New York, New York 10020

WALLABY and colophon are trademarks
of Simon & Schuster

First Wallaby Books Printing May, 1981

10 9 8 7 6 5 4 3 2 1

Manufactured in the United States of America

Library of Congress Catalogue Card Number: 80-26502

ISBN: 0-671- 42308-8

The advice in this book is based on careful research
and analysis. Due care should be taken in any repair
or maintenance program. The author and publisher
cannot take any responsibility for damage or injuries
caused by repairs or maintenance performed by
the reader.

Production: Jeffrey Weiss Group, Inc./Color Book Design, Inc.
Series Editor: Edward P. Stevenson
Design: Deborah Bracken, Design Director
Design Consultant: Robert Luzzi
Managing Editor: Barbara Frontera
Copy Chief: Donna Florence
Illustrated by: Jim Silks and Randall Lieu
Special Thanks to Jack Artenstein, Eugene Brissie, Jenny Doctorow and
Channa Taub

Table of Contents

Introduction

Wallcoverings and some minimal skills are all you need to give your house a new look. Gone are the days when wallpapering meant grandmother's cabbage roses that, once put up, were difficult to take down. The new products not only go up easily and are easy to care for, but are also easy to remove and replace when you feel like redecorating. In addition to the traditional wallpaper in a variety of patterns, today's wallcoverings include vinyl, murals, grass cloths, cork and fabric.

They serve many purposes. You can use wallcovering to dramatize one area of a room, to highlight recessed nooks and window niches, or to create a completely new look with coordinated fabrics for furniture covers and curtains. You can decorate an old screen, redo old cabinets or furniture, or put up an instant bulletin board in your child's room by lining a wall with cork.

This book will give you an overall look at the world of wallcoverings. It will tell you about the materials available and the qualities that make some of them especially suitable for certain projects. It will list the tools you will need, and give specific instructions for completing any job from start to finish.

Wallcoverings offer one of the easiest and least expensive ways to redecorate, and you can learn to do the job as well as most professionals.

So use your imagination and have fun!

A Wealth of Choices

Your main consideration when selecting wallcoverings will be your decorating theme. You will of course want to choose colors and patterns that suit your furniture and contribute to the atmosphere you have in mind for each room. But there are other factors you should consider when you start looking at samples: Is the wallcovering easy to work with? Is it durable? Washable? Does it come off easily when you want to redecorate? A wallcovering suitable for your living room might not be practical for your bathroom or kitchen. Let's take a look at the various types of wallcoverings available and their properties so that you can think about your needs before you go to your wallpaper dealer.

Standard Wallpapers

Standard wallpapers are either machine- or hand-printed and come in a wide variety of colors and patterns. Hand-printed or silk-screened papers often come with an edging (selvage) that must be trimmed before they are hung. Machine-printed papers are almost always pretrimmed and therefore require less work. A number of wallpapers are also available "pre-pasted"—with a dry, factory-applied paste on the back—which means less work for you because you merely wet them and apply them to the wall. If the paper is not pre-pasted, you must buy the appropriate paste from your dealer. You'll learn more about pastes later in this section.

Recommended Uses: Standard wallpaper is a good choice for low-traffic areas where soil or fingerprints won't be a problem, such as living rooms, dining rooms, adult bedrooms or studies.

Vinyl and Vinyl-coated Wallpapers

Vinyl papers are probably the most popular of the do-it-yourself wall-coverings. They are very durable, soil-resistant and washable, and come in an ever-widening range of patterns and colors.

• Solid vinyl papers are by far the more durable and scrubbable of the two—they are slightly more expensive but well worth it for a long-term installation.

• Vinyl-coated papers—standard "fiber-based" papers with a thin layer of clear vinyl on the surface—are economical and washable but not as resistant to wear and tear as solid vinyls. Most standard papers made in this country are vinyl-coated.

Both vinyl and vinyl-coated papers are available pre-pasted. If you choose ready-to-paste (not pre-pasted) vinyls, buy the appropriate paste at the same time. However, if this is your first wallpapering project, do consider pre-pasted papers. In addition to being easy to work with, they are generally peelable or strippable, which means they are easy to remove.

Recommended Uses: Solid vinyls are great for the entire house, and are ideal for areas such as kitchens, bathrooms and children's rooms. Vinyl-coated papers are suitable for medium-traffic areas such as hallways or bedrooms.

Foils

Foils are very thin wallcoverings made of simulated metal or aluminum laminated onto the surface of paper. They have a highly dramatic mirror finish and come in a variety of colors—some solid, most in bold, striking patterns.

Foils tend to be expensive and must be handled very carefully: once wrinkled, they can't be smoothed out. Because they are so thin and have a reflective surface which highlights any imperfections in the wall underneath, they must be applied over a perfectly smooth surface, preferably one pre-lined with blank wallpaper stock. Foils are hung with the same type of paste as vinyl papers. Your dealer will advise.

Recommended Uses: Foils can be difficult to work with, but are a superb decorating aid for any room— from living room to bathroom— where you want a bold, dramatic touch.

Flocked Wallpapers

Flocked wallpapers have a raised pattern produced by applying nylon or rayon fibers over imprinted paper, vinyl or foil. The effect is similar to that of cut velvet or damask fabrics.

Flocked wallpaper is elegant and generally expensive. While it may be washable, the flock is easily damaged by rubbing. Most flocks come ready-for-pasting (not prepasted), so buy the appropriate paste at the same time. Care must be taken not to damage or flatten the nap on flocks during hanging.

Recommended Uses: Flocks can enhance living rooms and dining rooms where the decorating theme is one of traditional elegance.

Grass Cloth, Burlap and Hemp

Natural-textured wallcoverings make an excellent backdrop for today's decors and have become very popular. They are generally mounted on a paper backing and are put up with wheat paste or cellulose, but some are available prepasted and are peelable. They are all fairly easy to hang because there are no patterns to be matched. It is important, however, that they be put up on a smooth surface, preferably one pre-lined with a blank wallpaper stock (see Preparing Your Walls, p.18).

The prices of natural-textured weaves range from quite reasonable to expensive. Burlap is the best buy of the three, both because of its cost and because rolls of burlap are more uniform in color than rolls of grass cloth or hemp, so that joins are less noticeable. Some burlaps are washable. Grass and hemp are not.

Recommended Uses: Any room relatively free of soil, grease or moisture. Burlap doesn't show tack marks, and is very practical for walls where you want to hang pictures or posters.

Matched Paper and Fabric

Matched or coordinated wallpaper and fabrics used to be a designer's prerogative but are now available at reasonable prices. They can turn even the dullest room into an enchanting one. Some of these wallcoverings come with matching bed linens, quilts, wall hangings, curtains and other accessories. The wallpapers may be standard or vinyl, pre-pasted or ready-to-paste. If you are handy with a sewing machine or know someone who is, you can use the coordinated fabric to make curtains, slipcovers, tablecloths, pillow covers and shower curtains—the range of applications is as wide as your imagination.

Recommended Uses: Any room in the house that needs a total facelift. Choose a vinyl wallpaper if you're going to do a kitchen, bathroom or children's room.

Murals

Murals are large scenic or geometric designs cut up into wallpaper-width strips that come in roll form, just like standard papers. The individual strips are all part of one big design rather than a repeating pattern. Both geometric and scenic designs are available in a wide variety of sizes and colors. An abstract geometric pattern may be just the thing to brighten your modern playroom or children's room, while a scenic mural—a seascape or a country landscape—can give special interest and depth to your living room and dining area.

Prices of murals vary widely depending on whether they are machine printed, hand-silk-screened or lithographed. The procedure for hanging them will depend on their backing material and whether or not they are pre-pasted. As for all other types of wallcoverings, the surface must be carefully prepared before installation.

Recommended Uses: Use murals where a strong focal point is needed (or wanted). Some murals are vinyl-coated and washable, while others are not practical for high-traffic areas. Compare the prices and properties of various murals before you decide which one is best for the area you have in mind.

Staple-on Fabrics

Professional decorators responsible for creating interior settings and displays in department stores and television studios have long relied on a staple gun and fabric as a quick and economical shortcut to decorating a room.

Staple-on fabrics don't have the permanence of other wallcoverings, but that in itself can be a plus if you want to redecorate a bedroom or dining area every couple of years. The walls need little if any preparation before the fabric is attached. While many fabrics are costly, others are inexpensive to work with. "Decorator" sheets make great staple-on fabrics—they come in a wide range of designer patterns and colors at relatively low prices.

Recommended Uses: Any room, wall or area that needs an instant and temporary decorating touch.

Where to Buy Wallcoverings

Your local paint and wallpaper dealer carries a large selection of the most popular wallpapers, and you'll also find wallcoverings in home-improvement stores. Virtually every department store has a wallpaper section. You may also want to check mail-order catalogs: both J.C. Penney and Sears, Roebuck, for instance, carry a wide range of economical wallcoverings including vinyls, corks, burlaps, murals and matching wallpapers and fabrics. More exotic wallcoverings, such as designer wallpaper, are available through interior decorating shops.

How Much to Buy

O nce you've decided on the kind of wallcovering to use, you'll want to make sure you get enough material to complete the job. Not only is it inconvenient and annoying to run out of supplies in the middle of the job, but since different batches of wallcoverings may vary slightly in color and texture, you should get all the material you need at the same time to make sure it matches. Most wallpaper dealers will take back, for a full refund, any unopened rolls you have left over. (It is a good policy to ask about this policy beforehand, though.)

How to Measure

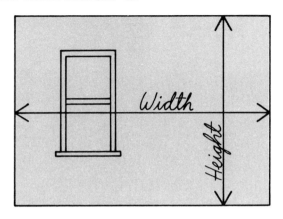

Wallcoverings come in rolls. They may vary in width (from paper to paper) from 18 to 54 inches, but each "single" roll contains exactly 36 square feet of material. Most papers are available in single and double (72 square-foot) rolls. A few may be available in triple (108 square-foot) rolls. To determine how many rolls of material you need, you will first have to measure the size (surface area) of the walls you plan to cover.

When measuring the surfaces to be covered, it will help to make a rough sketch of each wall, including windows and other openings. As you measure, enter the dimensions on the sketch:

1. Measure the height and width (in feet) of each wall.

2. Multiply the width by the height to get the area of the wall (in square feet).

3. Add together the surface areas of all the walls.

You now have the total surface area of the room. However, this includes doors, windows and other surfaces such as fireplaces which should be subtracted from the total.

1. Measure the height and width (in feet) of each door, window and other opening or surface you do not plan to cover.

2. Multiply the height by the width to find the area of each not-to-be-covered wall section, and add the resulting figures together. This represents the area, in square feet, of all the surfaces not to be covered.

When you subtract the total not-to-be-covered area from the total surface area, you have the total area (in square feet) to be covered.

Allowing for Repeats

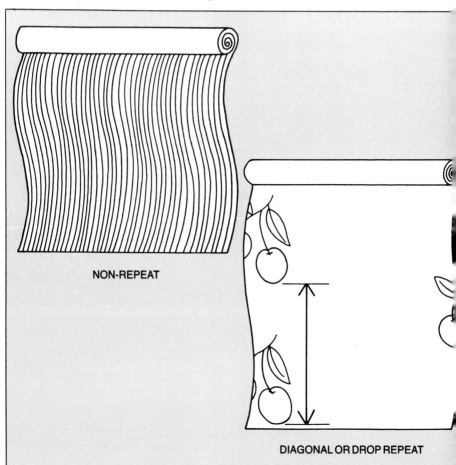

NON-REPEAT

DIAGONAL OR DROP REPEAT

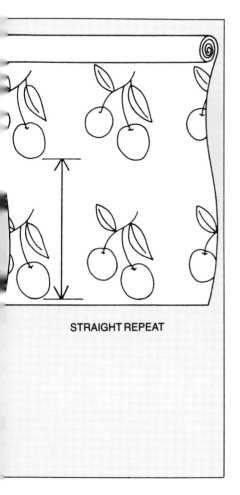

STRAIGHT REPEAT

A pattern repeat is the number of inches between the beginning of any pattern and the beginning of the next. Most manufacturers list the pattern repeat of the wallcovering in their sample book.

If you are using a paper with a long repeat, it will help to figure out how many pattern repeats will fit on your wall, thereby getting a more accurate fix on the amount of waste.

To figure waste due to pattern repeat, follow these three steps:

1. Divide the height of the wall by the number of inches between pattern repeats. *If you get a fraction, round up to the next whole number.*

2. Now multiply the pattern repeat by the number you just got.

3. If the result of this multiplication is larger than your wall height, the difference represents the extra inches you will need for each strip you hang.

For example: if your wall is 96 inches high and the repeat pattern is 19 inches, dividing 96 by 19 gives you 5.05. Rounding up to 6 and multiplying by 19 you get 114 inches. So the 19 inch pattern will fit 5 times with 18 inches of waste for each strip.

Measuring Tips

- USE A STEEL TAPE MEASURE SO YOU CAN MEASURE IN A STRAIGHT LINE.

- ALWAYS ROUND UP TO THE NEXT NEAREST FOOT (e.g., 6 feet, 7 inches = 7 feet).

- IF OPPOSITE WALLS ARE OF EQUAL SIZE, DON'T MEASURE THEM TWICE, BUT DO MEASURE THE OPENINGS IN EACH.

- INSTEAD OF MEASURING DOORS AND WINDOWS, YOU CAN SIMPLY SUBTRACT 15 to 20 SQUARE FEET (½ to ⅔ of a roll) FOR EACH AVERAGE-SIZED OPENING.

- IF YOU'RE COVERING THE CEILING, YOU CAN MEASURE THE SURFACE AREA AT FLOOR LEVEL.

- TAKE YOUR SKETCHES AND MEASUREMENTS TO YOUR DEALER. ONCE YOU HAVE SELECTED A WALLCOVERING, HE WILL HELP YOU DETERMINE EXACTLY HOW MUCH MATERIAL YOU'LL NEED.

How Many Rolls, Please?

Once you have figured the total surface area to be covered, you can determine how many rolls of paper you will need. Theoretically, to get the number of rolls, you would simply divide the number of square feet of surface by 36 (each roll of wallpaper contains 36 square feet of material, remember?). BUT, you will always need some extra material because:

- Some will be wasted during trimming and cutting.

- Matching of patterns may result in additional waste.

- You may want extra material for outlet covers or valances and for future repairs.

- There's always a chance that a strip of material may be damaged in handling and will need replacing.

So, as a rough guide, you should figure on getting more or less 30 square feet of *usable* paper from each single roll. To get a more realistic estimate of the number of rolls needed, divide the total surface area by 30. If you get a fraction, round up to the next nearest whole number. Even with this apparently generous waste allowance, it is wise to add an extra 10 to 20 percent to your order, to cover contingencies. (Remember, again, that most dealers will take back any unopened rolls.)

How Much Adhesive

Adhesives, usually referred to as pastes, come in a ready-to-mix form generally made from wheat flour and in pre-mixed varieties made

from synthetic materials. There are a number of adhesives on the market, each designed for a specific application. Here are some guidelines for what to use, where, and how much.

- **Dry pastes,** which must be mixed, have a higher water content than pre-mixed pastes. They should be used only on porous coverings such as standard papers or fabrics. One pound of dry mix is usually enough to hang six to eight rolls of paper. Follow label instructions for dry mix. Be careful not to make the paste too thin.

- **Pre-mixed vinyl adhesives** (that is, adhesive designed for hanging vinyl papers) should be used for nonporous coverings such as vinyls and foils. One gallon of vinyl adhesive is enough to hang 2 to 4 rolls of wallpaper. Different types of vinyl adhesives are available, including a vinyl-to-vinyl adhesive for overlapped joints.

Preparing Your Walls

O ne of the key trade secrets to a professional-looking job is a well-prepared surface. Wall preparation may be time-consuming, but it is worth doing right. The following section tells you what tools to use and how to prepare the wall, depending on its type and condition, and on the type of covering you're planning to apply.

Tools You May Need

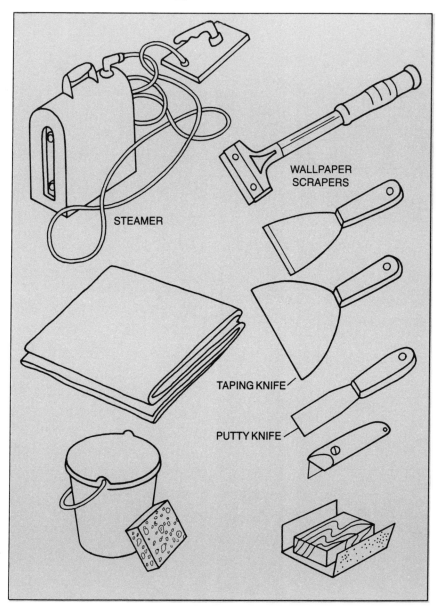

STEAMER

WALLPAPER SCRAPERS

TAPING KNIFE

PUTTY KNIFE

Removing Wall Fixtures

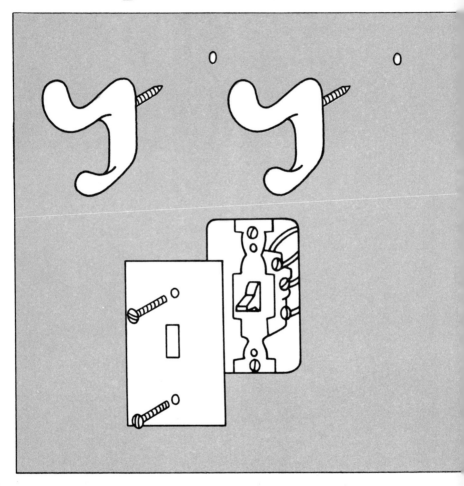

1. First, clear the wall of electrical outlets and switch plates and other impediments.

2. Remove picture hooks, nails, curtain rods and other hangings. The holes these leave will have to be filled.

Old Wallpaper

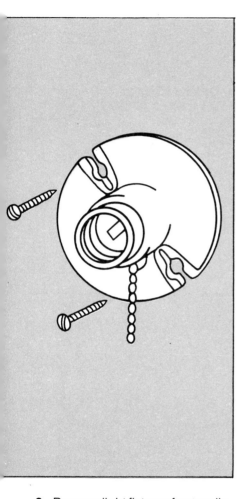

In general, a better job will result if all old wallcoverings are removed before new wallpaper is hung. *If* there is only a single layer of porous material (i.e., paper as opposed to vinyl, etc.) adhering tightly to the wall and without any texture, it may safely be left on. Old paper *must* be removed when:

- The old wallcovering is flocked, grass or other textured fabric which would show through under the new covering.

- The old wallcovering is vinyl, foil or other nonporous material to which the new covering would not adhere.

- The new covering will be vinyl, foil or other nonporous material which will not allow the new paste to evaporate and might loosen the old covering.

3. Remove light fixtures from walls (and ceilings if you are covering ceilings). You can paper around a fixture (we'll tell you how later), but the job is easier and comes out looking better if you remove the fixture.

Papering Over

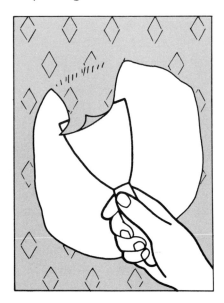
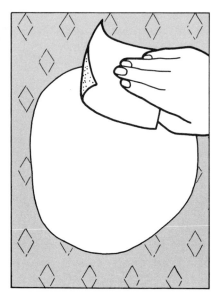

If you leave the old wallpaper on the wall, you may still have to go through a few preparatory steps before you hang the new wallcovering:

1. Scrape off any loose material and "feather" the remaining edges with fine sandpaper.

2. Puncture any air bubbles, cut an X in the material and paste down the flaps.

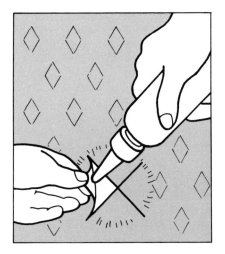

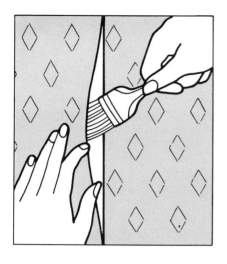

3. Look for loose seams and joints, including those in the corners, and paste them down.

4. Fill all holes and cracks with spackle or patching plaster and sand them when dry.

Removing Strippable Paper

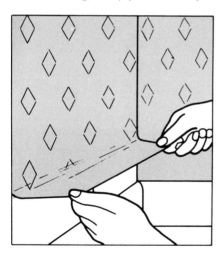

The existing wallpaper may be one of the strippable or peelable kinds. If so, the job will be fairly easy since the covering is *made* to be removable.

1. Begin with one strip of paper, pry up one bottom corner, and gently pull strip away from the wall.

2. When all the paper has been removed, cover the furniture and floors near the wall with protective drop cloths.

3. Wash the walls with a solution of household cleaner, which you can buy at your paint or hardware store. Rinse thoroughly and allow to dry.

Removing Non-strippable Paper

If your old wallpaper is not strippable, it will have to be scraped off and your job will be a little more difficult. Two methods are commonly used to make the task easier: the wallpaper steamer or chemical remover. The principle is the same with both—the steam or chemical is applied to the surface for as long as it takes to loosen the old adhesive so the covering can be scraped off easily. In either case:

- Nonporous coverings should be perforated so that the steam or chemical can reach the old adhesive underneath.

- If there is more than one layer of paper on the wall, try removing one at a time. You'll find that some layers come off more easily than others.

When scraping be careful; try not to gouge holes or scratches in the wall.

CAUTION: DO NOT ALLOW WATER OR CHEMICALS TO ENTER ELECTRICAL OPENINGS.

Using a Steamer

A wallpaper steamer can be rented by the day from most paint or wall-paper dealers. The unit consists of an electrically powered steam generator connected by a hose to a wall plate. While steaming is a slightly more costly method than chemical removal, it is generally more efficient. Proceed as follows:

- Cover the furniture and floors with protective drop cloths.

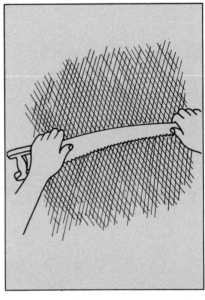

- Perforate the wallpaper if it isn't porous. You can use a perforating roller, or a wood saw drawn across the paper in random directions does an excellent job; or use any other tool that you have handy.

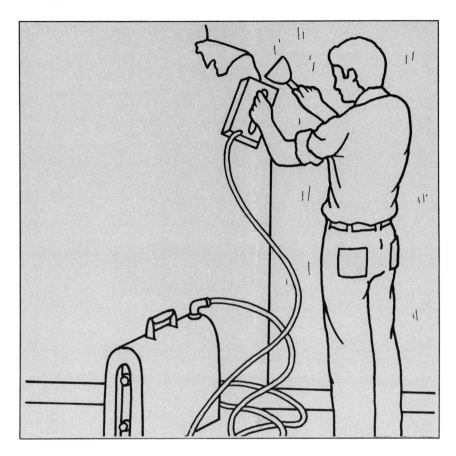

- Work on one strip at a time, applying the steamer wall plate to the wall with one hand and scraping paper off with a putty knife or scraper in the other hand.

You can work either from the top down or from the bottom up, depending on the type of steamer and the condition of the wallpaper. The object is to get as much moisture under the paper as possible. Starting at the top will allow the steam to condense and roll down the wall. Starting at the bottom will allow the steam to rise and seep into the paper. Try both methods and see which works better for you.

Using Chemical Removers

- Cover the furniture and floors with protective drop cloths.

- Apply chemical to the wallpaper with a sponge. Start at the top so that excess chemical will flow *down* the wall.

  Note: It is a good idea to wear rubber gloves when working with chemical solutions. Avoid splashing, especially into your eyes.

- When paper starts to loosen, carefully scrape it off with a putty knife or wallpaper scraper.

- Mix a solution of household cleaner and wash the wall thoroughly, then rinse it with clear water. Allow to dry overnight.

Patch and Plaster

The smoother the surface, the better your final wallcovering job will look. Here are some techniques for repairing cracks and holes in wallboard and plaster.

Small Holes and Cracks

These are easily repaired with spackle (also known as spackling compound) and a small flexible putty knife. Remove all loose material from the hole or crack, dampen it, and then using the putty knife, fill it with one smooth stroke. When filling a nail hole, let the spackle project above the surface since it will shrink as it dries. When the filler is dry, sand it smooth and flat, using medium-grit sandpaper.

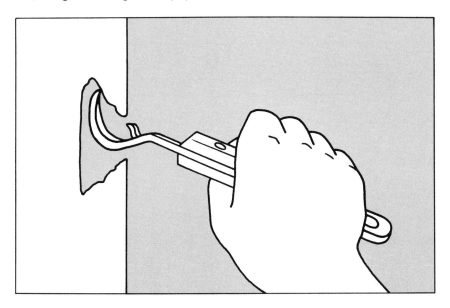

Hairline cracks should be widened before filling so that the patching material has a better hold. Use a razor knife for wallboard, and a pointed tool such as a can opener for plaster, and enlarge the hairline crack to an inverted V shape. Fill the crack using a putty knife and spackle. When the filler is dry, sand it smooth.

Large Holes and Cracks

Larger holes in plaster or wallboard will require a different approach. The specific materials and techniques will depend on the particulars of the case in question.

For Lath and Plaster Walls

Where the lath is more or less intact, it will be necessary to build up several layers of the patching material. (The material marketed as "patching plaster"—as opposed to plaster of Paris or spackle—is best for this sort of job.)

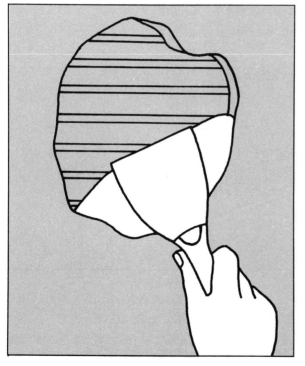
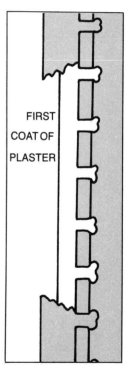

FIRST
COAT OF
PLASTER

- Clean out any loose material and dampen all surfaces with water.

- Mix a small amount of patching plaster and apply a base coat to the wounded wall, working from the edges to the center. Don't try to make the patch flush with the wall surface yet.

- Let the first layer dry thoroughly, then dampen the surface as before and apply another layer. Depending on the depth and width of the hole, the process may have to be repeated two or three times, or until the filler is at least level with the surrounding surface.

  - When the final layer is dry, sand it smooth and flat with medium sandpaper wrapped around a small block of wood.

Where the lath is broken or absent, it will be necessary to provide some substitute surface to support the patching material.

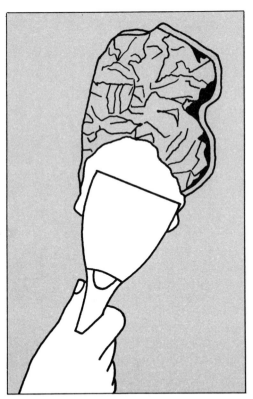 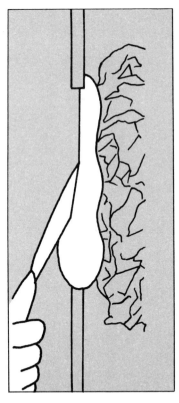

- One simple method is simply to stuff the opening with wadded newspaper or coarse steel wool, and apply the first coat of filler over the stuffing. Additional layers of filler are added until the area is at least level with the surrounding wall.

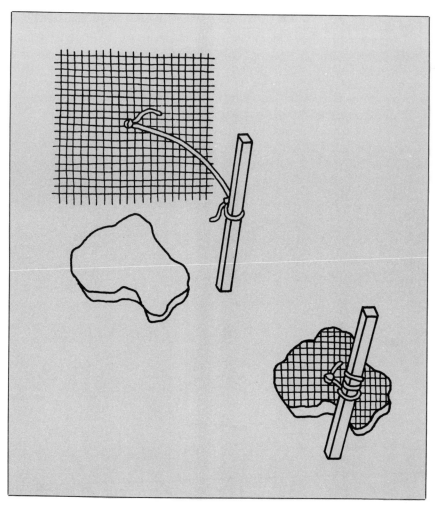

- Another method is to cut a piece of wire screen slightly larger than the hole. Tie a piece of string to the center of the screen and tie the other end of the string to a stick somewhat longer than the width of the hole. Push the screen through the opening and with the string pull it tight against the back surface of the plaster. The stick will prevent the screen's falling out of place if the string is twisted like a tourniquet until moderately tight. A first layer of patching plaster is applied, as above. When it is dry, the string is cut off flush, and additional layers of filler are applied as needed.

For Wallboard

Most repairs in gypsum wallboard involve the use of joint tape, a strong paper tape about three inches wide, and joint compound, a plaster-like compound designed especially for use in joining the seams between panels.

Patch a large crack (a typical repair) as follows:

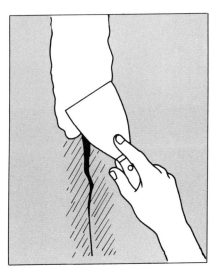

- Tear off a length of joint tape slightly longer than the crack.

- Using a four-inch putty knife, known as a "taping" knife, spread a band of joint compound along the crack area wide enough to accommodate the tape.

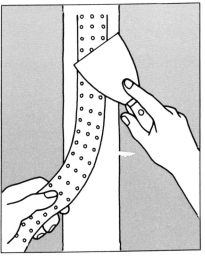

- Lay the tape over the band of joint compound and press it firmly into place by running the taping knife over it.

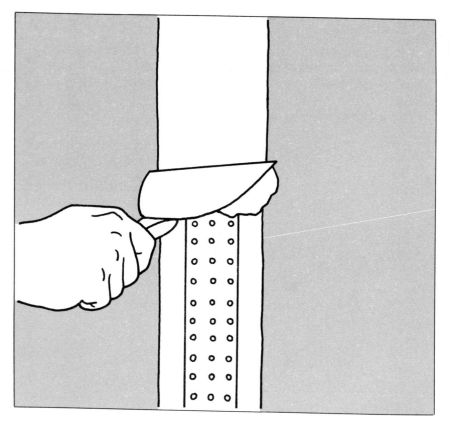

- Put another layer of joint compound *over* the tape, carefully smoothing or "feathering" the edges down. Allow the whole area to dry, sand lightly, and apply another coat of compound so that it extends an inch or two past the previous coat on either side. Sand smooth when dry.

Note: The final smoothing or "feathering" may be done with a damp sponge rather than sandpaper. This method is a bit neater, but don't overdo it. You can wash away all the compound if you are not careful.

To patch a large hole in wallboard, you must cut a patch out of scrap wallboard to replace the missing material. Besides the scrap, you will need special wallboard clips, a small saw, joint tape and joint compound. The repair is made as follows:

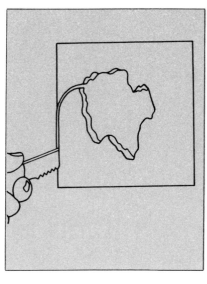

- Using the small saw, cut a patch somewhat larger than the hole.

- Place the patch over the hole and trace its outline in pencil on the wall.

- Cut out around the penciled outline so that the patch will fit snugly.

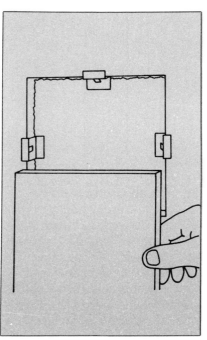

- Using the special clips, slip the patch into place in the hole.

- Cover the joint between the patch and the rest of the wall with joint tape and joint compound.

Popped Nails

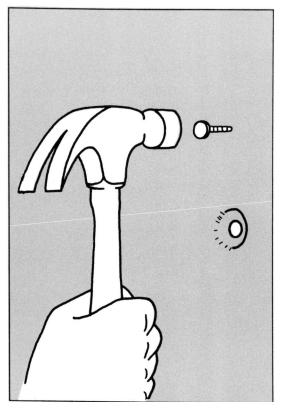
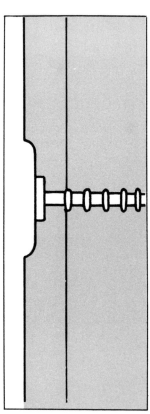

The nails that hold wallboard panels against the wall studs often loosen during the normal course of wear and tear, "popping" out from the wall surface. Take care of this problem by first hammering the nail gently but firmly back into its original position. The face of the hammer should drive the head of the nail between $\frac{1}{32}$ and $\frac{1}{16}$ of an inch below the surface of the wallboard and leave a gentle depression around the nail head which will later be filled in with joint compound. Next, to secure the wallboard more firmly, drive a special "threaded" or annular ringed wallboard nail about three inches above or below the popped nail, setting it carefully just below the surface as before. Fill the indentations with joint compound. It will probably take two or three coats to get a perfectly flush, smooth result. Sandpaper if necessary.

Preparing Surfaces

Prime and Seal

Any new wall surface—and that includes patched and repaired sections as well as new plaster or wallboard walls—needs to be primed and sealed before any other finishing operation is carried out. The purpose of priming and sealing is to limit the absorbency of the wall surface and keep adhesives and other finishes *on* the wall surface, not *in* it.

Seal new wall surface areas with one or two coats of any commercial oil-based or water-based (often known as "PVA") primer sealer, applied with brush and/or roller. Allow the primer coats to dry thoroughly.

It used to be standard practice to "size" a wall before applying wallpaper. Sizing involves painting a coat of animal glue or similar substance on the wall to improve the adhesion of the paste. Sizing has largely been outmoded by developments in wallpaper paste composition. If it should be required, either your wallpaper dealer or the instructions that come with the wallpaper (or both) should advise you of that fact clearly. Size, a powdered preparation much like wallpaper paste, is easy to apply. Follow manufacturer's instructions.

Pre-Papering with Blank Stock

Application of a smooth backing or lining material to the wall is recommended as a foundation for the final finished wallcovering in some instances, most notably in the case of foil papers that mercilessly reveal any imperfections in the wall surface underneath. Such blank stocks—unprinted, textureless wallpapers or fabrics—are available from all wallpaper dealers.

Hanging a blank stock is exactly like hanging a finished wallpaper. The surface of the blank stock is designed to provide the best adhesion for pastes, so further sealing or sizing should be unnecessary. Your dealer should be able to provide you with any further information you might need about blank stocks.

Hanging the Wallcovering

Now that you're ready to hang your wallcovering, you probably can't wait to see how that first strip will look on your wall. But be sure you have everything you need before you start. A few preparations will save you unnecessary interruptions and will protect your furniture and floors.

- First put on some old work clothes.

- Next move all the furniture into the middle of the room, or, if you're wallpapering the ceilings, move the lighter pieces out of the room.

- Cover the floors and furniture in the room with drop cloths to protect them from water and adhesive.

- Now get all the tools you need so they will be readily available.

Tools

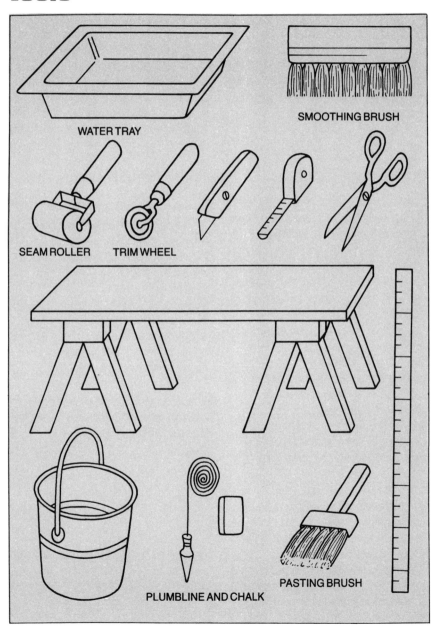

WATER TRAY

SMOOTHING BRUSH

SEAM ROLLER   TRIM WHEEL

PLUMBLINE AND CHALK   PASTING BRUSH

The exact tools you'll need will depend on whether you're using pre-pasted or ready-to-paste wallcovering, and the degree to which you can improvise. Most of the special tools you'll need can be bought as an inexpensive kit from your wallpaper dealer if you don't already have them in the house.

More About Tools

A work surface for cutting and pasting the wallcovering can range from a special *paste table,* which you can rent, to a clean and protected floor area. Whatever surface you use, make sure you have an area at least six feet by three feet. Two card tables may do.

If you're using ready-to-paste wallcoverings, you can apply the paste with a *paste brush* and *bucket* or *paint roller* and *roller tray.* For pre-pasted wallcoverings, you'll need a specially made or improvised *water tray.* In either case you should have *an extra bucket and sponge* with clear water to clean up excess paste.

You'll always need a *flexible metal tape measure* to measure wall areas and wallcovering material. A *straightedge* will help in cutting and trimming strips.

A *chalkline* will be needed to give you a true vertical line, and can be constructed from a length of string, a heavy weight and colored chalk.

A straightedge used with a carpenter's level will give you the same result with a little more work.

You'll need *scissors* or a *utility knife* to cut and trim wallcoverings. There are also special trimming wheels, either perforated or knife-edged, to trim coverings. A razor holder will also do for trimming, and a triangular trimming guide will help to hold down and flatten coverings as you trim.

To smooth down most standard coverings a *long bristled brush,* 12 inches wide, should be used. There are special shorter-bristled brushes for vinyl. Most pre-pasted coverings can be smoothed down with a *sponge.*

Unless you're unusually tall, you'll need a *stepladder* or *stool* to reach the top of the wall. Make sure whatever you use is steady. If you're covering the ceiling, a scaffold made from two stepladders and some planks will be very helpful.

A *seam roller* will be needed to smooth down the edges where two strips of wallcovering meet.

Deciding Where to Start

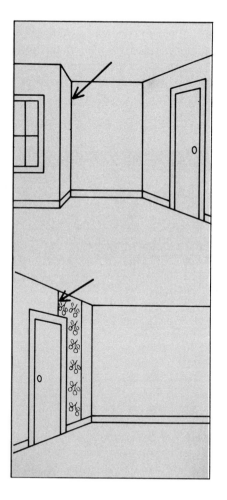

Laying out a game plan for applying your wallcovering is important whether you are covering one wall or an entire room. Following are some general guidelines:

Note: If you are covering the ceilings as well as the walls, do the ceilings first. (For purely practical reasons, we will discuss how to do this later.)

- If you are covering a room without any built-ins, such as a fireplace or bookcase, start and finish in the most inconspicuous area because patterns will generally not match exactly where the first and last piece meet. Good inconspicuous areas are the narrow wall above a door, a dimly lit alcove, a corner hidden by an open door or any corner.

- If there is a natural break in the room, such as a built-in floor-to-ceiling closet, start on one side of it and finish on the other. If, however, one wall contains the focal point of the room— such as a picture window or a fireplace—you may want to start with that wall and work around from each side to the most inconspicuous area of the room.

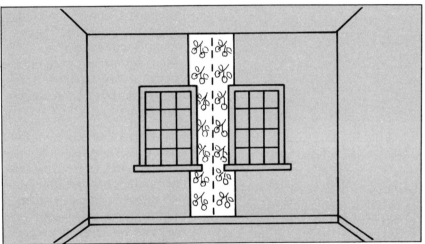

Here's how: Say your wall has a picture window, or two windows, or a fireplace. Your first strip should be placed on the centerline above the picture window or the fireplace, or the centerline between the two windows. In this way the openings will be symmetrically framed by the wallcovering. There are two ways to position the first strip on the centerline:

• The edge of the first strip is positioned on the edge of the centerline.

• The middle of the first strip is positioned on the centerline.

Choose which of these two ways to hang the first strip by determining which of them will give you the wider strips at the corners. Follow these steps to determine your starting position:

1. Mark the centerline on the wall between the two windows or above and below the center of the picture window or fireplace.

2. Starting at the centerline, and using a roll of wallcovering as a measuring rod, determine the number of strips it would take to get from the centerline to the corner if you began with the edge of a roll on the centerline.

3. Now place the *center* of the roll of wallcovering on the centerline and determine the number of strips it would take to get to the corner.

4. Choose as your starting point the one which requires the fewest strips or—if the number is the same—gives you the wider strips at the corners.

After having determined the starting point, you will work first in one direction and then in the other, meeting in the least conspicuous area of the room, or to a natural break such as a built-in bookcase or closet.

Getting Things Straight

It is essential that wallcoverings be hung straight. Unfortunately, walls, corners, etc., are virtually never "true," that is vertical, perpendicular or square. We have to compensate, then, by establishing a true vertical line on each wall by which to align our paper. The technical term for true vertical is "plumb," and the easiest way to establish it is with a tool called a "plumbline" or "chalkline." This consists of a piece of string with a weight at one end (the weight is called a "plumb bob"). When the weight is suspended at the bottom of the string, gravity does the rest: the string describes a true vertical line. If the string is rubbed with colored chalk, it can be tensioned, after it has come to rest, and snapped against the wall to make a clear reference line. This procedure is carried out on each wall we will cover. Step by step, here is the way to "snap" a vertical chalk line.

- Attach a plumb bob or any non-bulky weight, such as a bolt, to one end of your chalkline (string).

- Chalk the line with colored powdered chalk (available at your hardware store).

- Lightly drive a tack into the wall, next to the ceiling, at the point where you want your reference line to be.

- Tie the chalkline to the tack, making sure the bob swings clear of the floor.

- When the bob comes to rest, tension the line by pulling down on the end, press the line firmly against the wall with your thumb, reach up with your free hand, and smartly snap the line against the wall, as if you were shooting an arrow from a bow. This should give you a clear and accurate vertical reference.

Ready-to-paste Wallcovering

Cutting

1. Measure the height of the wall. In measuring your wallcovering for cutting, you will use this measurement and add 2 inches at the top and bottom for trimming.

2. If your wallcovering has a repeating pattern, hold the covering against the wall to decide where you want to locate the beginning of the pattern in relation to the ceiling line. When you've decided which part of the pattern to start with, mark the ceiling and floor lines *lightly* on the covering, add the two-inch trimming allowance at each end and cut, using a straightedge and utility knife. (To make sure each additional strip is long enough to permit accurate pattern matching, cut the next strip before hanging the first.)

3. If your paper has no repeat, mark off the length needed to cover the wall (including the trimming allowance, top and bottom) on the wallcovering, and cut. You can either cut off enough strips to cover the first wall or cut one strip at a time.

4. If your covering has selvage, or an unpatterned edge, it must be trimmed before hanging. Use a straightedge and razor or utility knife to remove the selvage with a clean quick stroke. (it may be simplest to do this after pasting, when the strip is folded.)

Pasting

1. Mix your paste, following manufacturer's instructions.

2. Lay the first strip face down on the pasting table. (If you wish, you may place the second strip under the first so that any excess paste laps over onto the second strip.)

3. Starting at the top, brush a coat of paste on the top half of the first strip.
Note: Be sure not to miss or skip *any* small areas, or you will have "blisters" (unpasted spots) in your finished wallpaper.

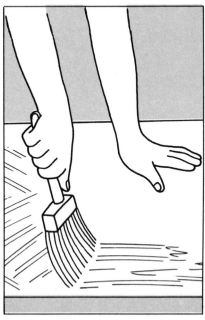

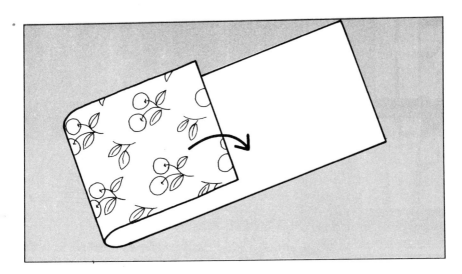

4. Now gently fold the pasted area over itself but *don't crease the covering at the fold.*

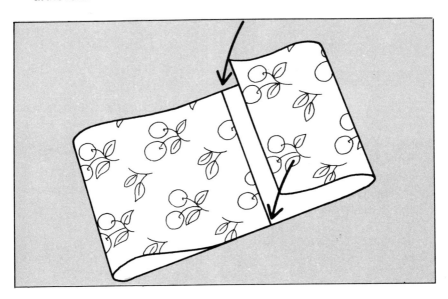

5. Paste the second half of the strip and carefully fold this half back on itself.

Hanging

1. Carry the strip to the wall, mount the ladder, unfold the top half, and press the covering into place locating the pattern (if any) properly in relation to the ceiling line, and lining the edge up with the chalk line.

2. Use the smoothing brush to stroke from the top down the center and from the center to the sides to force out air bubbles and excess paste and make the paper stick firmly to the wall. Work quickly, but don't rush.

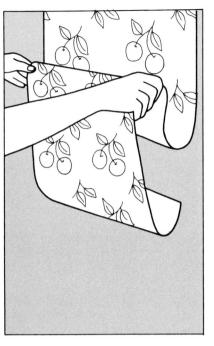

3. Once the top half has been smoothed into place, unfold the bottom half, line it up with the chalk line, and smooth it on as you did the top half. At this point, you will be able to slide the *entire* strip around as necessary in order to position it accurately. Be gentle!

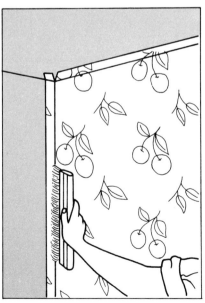

4. If you have started in a corner, make sure the covering extends for approximately an inch around the corner, and use the edge of the smoothing brush to tamp the paper firmly into the corner.

5. When the paper is smooth against the wall and all air bubbles (together with as much excess paste as possible) have been brushed out, use a trimming wheel or scissors point to score the covering along the ceiling and baseboard.

6. Now either lift the paper away from the wall and cut along the score line with scissors, or make the cut with a razor knife and a straightedge. Smooth the paper back onto the wall with the brush, brushing out all air bubbles as before.

7. Each subsequent strip is hung in exactly the same manner, with the pattern carefully matched, where that applies.

Hanging Prepasted Coverings

- Fill the water tray half-full with room-temperature water, and place it near the area to be covered.

- Cut the strip to the proper length (see Cutting, p. 43) and re-roll it with the pasted surface on the outside.

- Soak the strip in the water following manufacturer's recommendation as to time.

- Hang the strip on the wall sliding it into place accurately (see Hanging #3, above). A moist sponge can be used to smooth the covering down and to take up excess paste and water.

All other techniques are the same for pre-pasted as for ready-to-paste wallcoverings.

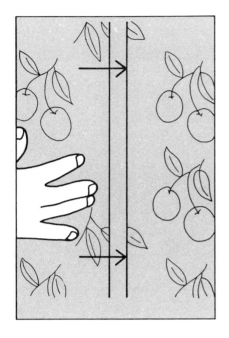

Making Seams

Since you want to make the seams of your wallcoverings unnoticeable, you will generally use butt joint seams. These are made by sliding one strip of paper against the other edge to edge until a *slight* ridge rises between the two strips. This ridge will disappear as the paste dries and the covering shrinks slightly. When the paste has begun to dry, use a seam roller to press the edges firmly against the wall. This will also force excess paste out of the seams.

Note: Be careful not to overdo the seam rolling—you can make the edges of the paper shiny if you press too hard. Do not use a seam roller at all on flocks. Instead use a damp cloth to press the seams firmly.

Special Techniques

Inside Corners

When you get to an inside corner, you must, in essence, start over again on the new wall, since the corner is almost certainly not true and plumb. This is done by dividing or "splitting" the next strip—the one that will turn the corner—vertically, and hanging each part of the strip independently, using the following procedure:

- When you get to less than a full strip's width from the corner, measure the distance from the edge of the previous strip to the corner in at least three places.

- Take the largest of these measurements, add two inches overlap to get around the corner and cut the strip vertically to this width, using scissors. It should be a fairly straight cut but needn't be perfect.

- Hang this partial strip, butting it against the previous strip and lapping it around the corner. Use the smoothing brush to tamp the paper into the corner.

- Measure the width of the remaining part of the strip.

- Measure that same distance out from the corner on the new wall and snap a vertical chalk line at that point.

- Hang the remainder of the divided strip, positioning it carefully along the chalk line. The two parts of the original, whole strip are now overlapped about two inches.

- Make a "double-cut" seam by cutting cleanly through both parts of the strip where they overlap and remove the trimmings. As one trimming will be underneath one of the resulting permanent panels, the edge of the top panel will have to be carefully peeled back, the trimming removed and the edge replaced and smoothed down again and the seam rolled.

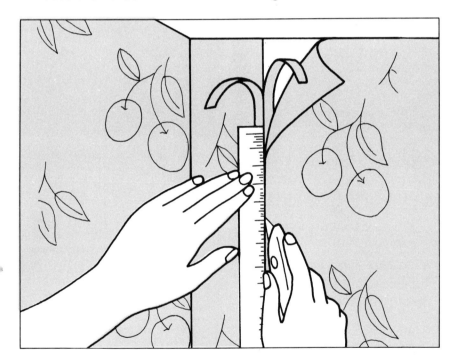

The cut for the double-cut seam may be made either freehand or with a straightedge, it doesn't much matter which on an inside corner. While the pattern will almost certainly not match accurately in this kind of a seam, the eye, distracted by the business of the pattern, is not likely to notice the discrepancy.

Outside Corners

The problem of outside corners is pretty much the same as for inside corners: the two walls are not likely to be plumb and the corner is not likely to be true. The solution is also very much the same. The strip that turns the corner will be "split" and the part that goes on the new wall will be hung to a new vertical chalk line and lapped back over the part that turned the corner. However,. unlike inside corners, the seams on outside corners tend to be more conspicuous. There are two approaches to dealing with this problem.

- One theory advises that the seam be made as close to the corner as possible—within ½" or so. To keep things neat, the cut for this double-cut seam should be made with the aid of a straightedge.

- The other theory suggests that the seam be kept as far from the corner as possible or that the corner-turning strip not be split at all, rather that a new strip be hung (properly aligned to its own vertical chalk line, of course) so as to overlap it slightly, and the double-cut seam be made there, again, using a straightedge to guide the knife.

Hanging Around Openings

Outlets

- Remove all cover plates as part of your wall preparation.

- Smooth the wallcovering over the opening.

- Carefully cut an X into the paper right up to the corners of the opening with a sharp razor or utility knife.

- Fold back flaps and trim along edge of opening.

- Smooth down edges with damp sponge or cloth.

Light Fixtures

- If you're removing the entire fixture, smooth the covering over the opening and trim as for outlet openings.

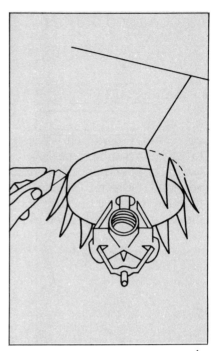

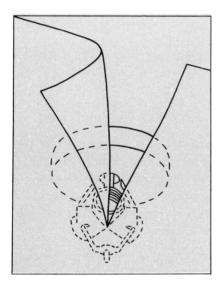

- If the fixture cover plate is in place, smooth the covering until you reach the fixture, and cut a straight line from one edge of the covering to the center of the fixture.

- Working gradually, cut slits in the covering that allow you to smooth the paper around the contour of the base of the fixture.

- Butt the edges of the straight cut together and carefully trim off excess paper around the fixture.

Immovable Objects

- If you come to an object such as a thermostat which cannot be removed, smooth the paper up to the edge of the fixture (as for light fixtures, above).

- Cut an X over the fixture, making it larger until the covering can be smoothed around the perimeter of the fixture.

- Carefully trim off excess with sharp razor knife.

Windows and Doors

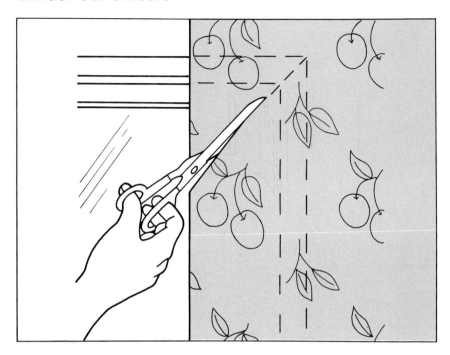

- When a strip of paper over-hangs a door or window open-ing, smooth the covering as close to the edge as possible without buckling the material.

- Cut a 45 degree diagonal to the corners of the opening and use edge of the smoothing brush to tap covering into the corner where the wall meets the win-dow or door frame.

- Trim excess with razor knife and straightedge.

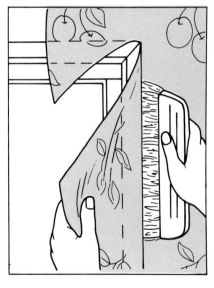

Recessed Windows

- If your windows are recessed and you want the inside surfaces papered, cover those surfaces first, lapping the paper over onto the wall about one inch. It will be necessary to slash to the point at which the paper makes its 90 degree bend.

- Then paper the wall surface as you would normally, either overlapping the edges of the recess paper or making a double-cut seam.

Ceilings

If you are covering the ceiling, do so before covering the walls. Unless there is a good reason not to, plan to hang your strips across the width rather than the length of the ceiling, since shorter strips are easier to hang than longer ones. First, make a reference line for hanging your first strip:

- From the end wall, measure out along *both* sides of the ceiling a distance equal to the width of the wallpaper minus one inch. Place a tack at each of these points.

- Tie a chalked string between the two tacks, pull it taut and snap it to create a guideline.

- Lay the first strip against this guideline; overlap the excess into the corner, and trim it off.

- Butt remaining strips against each other.

Ceilings will be easier to do if you have a scaffold and someone to help you.

Special Applications

Flocked Wallcoverings

Since flocked papers have a raised velvety design, you must be careful not to crush the flocking by using a seam roller or brushing too hard when smoothing the covering onto the wall. Also be careful not to get paste on the surface—if you do, wipe it off immediately with a damp sponge. Finish the job by brushing the covering gently in one direction so that the nap is raised.

Foil Wallcoverings

Foils must be handled very carefully to avoid folds, scratches and creases. Unlike other material, foil will not stretch or shrink, so when making butt joints with foils, do not ridge the seams but adjoin the edges carefully. It is generally recommended that walls be prepared with blank stock before hanging foils, and that vinyl adhesive be used to prevent mildew.

Hanging Fabrics

While fabrics can be applied to walls with adhesive in much the same way as ordinary wallcovering, stapling is a simple and effective alternative with several advantages. Walls do not need the extensive preparation required for ordinary wallcoverings—in fact, the staple-on techniques are ideal for hiding wall imperfections which are too time-consuming to repair. Also, stapled-on fabrics can be removed very easily and therefore make re-decorating a simple matter. This is handy if you move a lot or simply change your taste frequently. The staple-on technique is widely used by professionals for quick decorating and you can learn it easily.

Choosing Fabrics

Almost any kind of fabric can be used as a wallcovering, but bed sheets are particularly suitable because their size minimizes stapling and they are relatively inexpensive.

Stapling Tools

A *staple gun* is really all you need, but depending on the job you might also want a *screwdriver* or staple remover, *white glue,* and *single edge razor blades.* An *iron* is helpful too.

Staple guns range from heavy to light weight, and your choice should be determined by what feels comfortable for the size and strength of your hand. Depending on the gun, staples are available in lengths from 3/10 to 9/16 of an inch. The length of the staples should depend on the material you're stapling into. If the staple gun is not driving the staples flush with the wall surface, switch to a shorter staple length.

There are basically two methods of stapling fabrics to walls: flat stapling for attaching large single panels to an entire wall, and back-tacking for mounting several strips side by side, to cover an entire room.

Flat Stapling

Since a single king-size flat sheet will cover a 9x9 foot wall, flat stapling will meet many of your decorating needs.

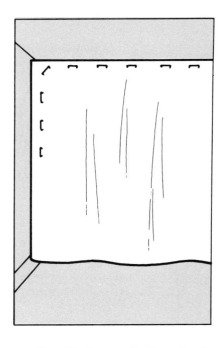

- Open the hems of both ends of the sheet and tack the sheet in position on the wall with "baste" staples. (Baste staples are simply those driven lightly into the wall so they can easily be removed for repositioning.)

- Once the sheet is positioned to your satisfaction, start stapling at the center of the left margin, first working up to the ceiling and then down to the floor as you stretch the fabric tightly.

- Stretch the fabric as taut as possible to the right wall and again start stapling at center and work up and down as you did on the left side.

- Pull the fabric tight against the ceiling and tack as close to the ceiling as possible while stretching.

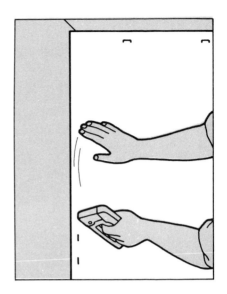

- Stretch the fabric toward the floor or baseboard and staple as far down as possible.

- Trim off excess on all four sides with a sharp razor blade, leaving a one inch hem allowance.

- Finish by turning raw edges under into a hem and iron flat.

- Run a bead of white glue underneath the hem and pat against the wall. Hold in place with masking tape until dry.

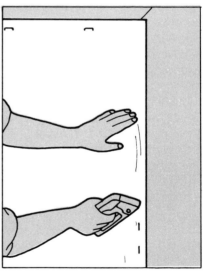

Hiding Staples

Depending on the material, the staples may or may not be visible. You can partially hide the staples by coloring the top of the staples with an appropriate colored marking pencil before loading them in the staple gun or after they are in place. The rows of staples can also be hidden by covering them with self-welting, upholsterer's tape, or borders cut to size from matching material, all of which may be attached along the border with white glue.

Back Tacking

If you're covering an entire room, back tacking provides a method that will hide all staples as you work. As with wallpapering, pick an inconspicuous corner of the room to start and finish.

- Cut the fabric into the required lengths, leaving 2 extra inches at top and bottom for trimming.

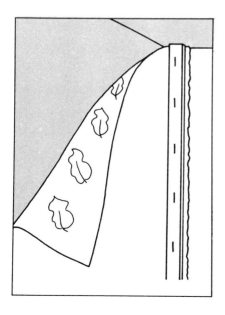

- Staple the left edge of the first panel into position, using upholsterer's tape along the back surface, (Upholsterer's tape is a thin strip of fairly rigid cardboard, used to give a clean edge to a folded fabric.)

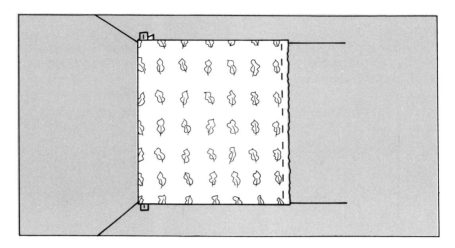

- Pull the panel taut to the right side and tack into place with broadly spaced staples. If you're using material with a bold pattern, it will help to align the right edge with a plumb line.

- Tack the top and then the bottom of panel into place as you stretch it tight.

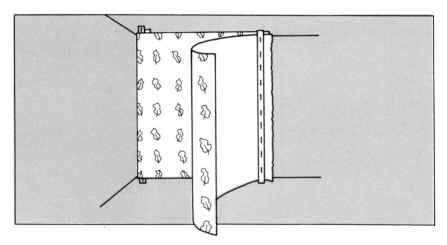

- Place the second panel face down over the first, matching for pattern repeats. Tack what is for the moment the right edge to hold it in place.

- Place a strip of upholsterer's tape along the right edge and *staple through the tape and both layers of fabric.*

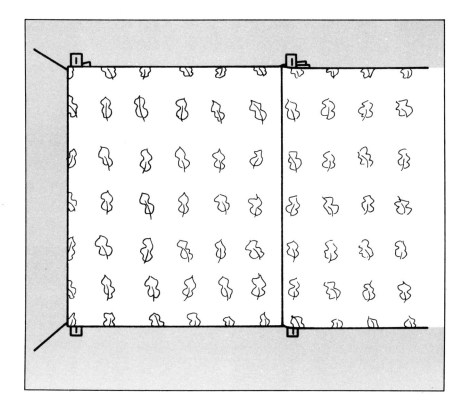

- Now turn the panel over and continue as before.

For the final panel:

- If you are simply completing a wall, cut the fabric to width, leaving a ½ inch hem allowance. Turn the hem under, press with an iron, and tack in place with staples.

- If you have come full circle and are meeting up with the very first panel, trim the fabric to width, as above, leaving a hem allowance. Turn and press the hem. Run a line of glue under the left-hand edge of the first panel and tuck the hemmed edge of the final panel behind that edge, using a piece of light cardboard to work it into place.

Top and bottom edges can either be trimmed flush and covered with molding, welting, coordinated borders or upholstery tape, or they can be hemmed and tacked with staples or held in place with a line of white glue.

The Wallaby Home Care Guides

How to Fix a Leak and Other Household Plumbing Projects

How to Redo Your Kitchen Cabinets and Counter Tops

How to Wallpaper

How to Paint Interiors

How to Build a Deck

How to Wire Electrical Outlets, Switches and Lights

The Wallaby Auto Care Guides

How to Tune Your Chevy Chevette

How to Tune Your Toyota Corolla